Thank you for giving failure a voice and for honouring the journey back to self.

If Phenomenal Women resonates, I'd be grateful for a short review or reflection:

https://amzn.eu/d/e1SnE2Q

Phenomenal Women

"How I Lost Myself - And Found the Fire to Rise Again"

Donn C. McCalla

Copyright © 2025 by Donn C. McCalla

All rights reserved.

No part of this publication may be reproduced, distributed, or transmitted in any form or by any means, including photocopying, recording, or other electronic or mechanical methods, without the prior written permission of the publisher, except in the case of brief quotations embodied in critical reviews or articles.

ISBN: Printed in the UK

First Edition

DEDICATION

For every woman who lost herself while loving someone else.

This is for you for the fire, for the silence, for the rise.

For Sharon, Natasha, and Claudia -

three beautiful, genuine souls whose hearts were made of love.

You were the kind of women who lit up the room, even when you were carrying pain no one else could see.

You smiled through it. You gave, even when you had little left for yourselves.

You loved fully, freely, and without condition.

Your strength was quiet, your grace unshakable.

And your joy pure, contagious, unforgettable.

You put others first, always.

And now, I put you first in these pages where your light lives on.

This book is for you.

Thank you for loving me.

Thank you for walking with me.

Thank you for being who you were.

Forever in my heart,

TABLE OF CONTENTS

Acknowledgements

- Gratitude for Support Along the Journey

Preface

- A Word Before You Begin (if applicable)

Introduction

- Reflections on Leaving: Choosing Peace Over Chaos

Part I: The Fire

1. The Illusion of Love
2. Realising Emotional Abandonment
3. The Courage to Walk Away
4. Reclaiming My Truth

Part II: The Rise
5. Rediscovering Joy
6. Setting Boundaries
7. Learning to Trust Myself Again
8. Rebuilding Self-Worth
9. Embracing Freedom and Authenticity

Part III: The Transformation
10. The Lasting Impact of Personal Growth
11. Embracing Full Potential
12. The Liberation of Living Authentically
13. Shifting Relationships
14. The Peace of Self-Acceptance

Themes

- Self-Worth and Authenticity
- Empowerment through Boundaries
- Transformation as a Journey
- Courage to Change
- Freedom in Self-Acceptance

Additional Features

- Quizzes and Journaling Prompts
- Affirmations and Exercises for Personal Growth

Conclusion

- Celebrating the Journey of Self-Love and Empowerment
- A Tribute to Women Rising, Healing, and Reclaiming Their Lives

Appendix

- Resources for Further Reading

About the Author

- Donn C. McCalla's Journey

Phenomenal Women - "How I Lost Myself – And Found the Fire to Rise Again"

Introduction

A woman doesn't always rise in fire.

Sometimes, she rises in silence

with clarity and grace.

There wasn't an explosion. No shouting. No drama. No tears.

Just peace and a quiet decision.

After 18 years, I walked away from a man who couldn't stop betraying me.

Not just through infidelity, but through a constant hunger for attention and admiration.

He needed validation like oxygen. He lived behind a charming mask, playing the life of the party. But beneath it, he was broken. And I knew it.

I told him that early on.

"You're damaged," I said, "but I don't need you I choose you."

And for nearly two decades, I stood by that choice.

Loyal. Steady. Strong. The one who held everything together.

And somehow, even through it all I didn't lose sight of who I was.

I knew about the cheating long before I left. But I waited until I was ready. I didn't leave for revenge. I didn't leave to punish him.

I left because it was time for me.

Quietly. Cleanly. With no mess. I simply said:

"Post my keys through the letterbox."

And that was it. I was done.

He didn't take it well.

He was angry not because he lost me, but because I didn't break.

Because I didn't scream, plead, or perform grief for his benefit.

I walked away with grace and integrity. And that, he couldn't handle.

I even asked my family not to speak poorly of him.

"This relationship isn't your business," I said. "Don't judge him. There'll be no retaliation from my side."

That's who I've always been. I don't let broken men turn me bitter.

But don't mistake my peace for softness.

I no longer let things slide. If it doesn't sit right, it's done.

I love fully, but never again at the cost of myself.

This is my story of knowing, of staying, of walking away without looking back.

Not as a victim, but as a woman who owns every inch of her truth.

This is for every woman who gave too much.

For every woman who tried to fix someone who didn't want to heal.

For every woman who's finally saying: no more.

This is Phenomenal Women – Phoenix Rises.

And this is how I rose from the fire, from the silence, from the truth.

Chapter 1: The Illusion of Love

Reflection Prompt/Quiz:

- **When did you first realise you were compromising your truth for love?**
- **What illusions about love have you held onto that need releasing?**
Write your thoughts below

Chapter 2: The Moment I Knew

Reflection Prompt/Quiz:

- What was the moment you knew something had to change?
- How did your body, mind, or spirit signal to you that a change was needed?
Reflect and journal your insights

Chapter 3: Rising from the Ashes

Reflection Prompt/Quiz:

- How did you rise from a place of pain or loss?
- What lesson did you learn in your "ash" that now guides your healing?
Take time to write your experience

Chapter 4: The Expectation

Reflection Prompt/Quiz:

- What expectations did you place on yourself or others?

- How did releasing or redefining these expectations allow you to grow?
  Reflect and journal your insights

Chapter 5: Learning to Trust Myself Again

Reflection Prompt/Quiz:

- What steps did you take to rebuild trust with yourself?
- What fears surfaced, and how did you face them?
  Reflect and journal your insights

Chapter 6: The Return of Joy

Reflection Prompt/Quiz:

- When was the last time you felt pure joy?
- What does joy look like in your life now?
  Reflect and journal your thoughts

Chapter 7: Opening the Door Again

Reflection Prompt/Quiz:

- What did opening your heart to new possibilities look like?
- How did you overcome fear and trust again?
Write your reflections

Chapter 8: Redefining Love

Reflection Prompt/Quiz:

- What has your understanding of love evolved into?
- How do you love yourself differently now?
Journal your thoughts

Chapter 9: Peace After the Storm

Reflection Prompt/Quiz:

- How did you find peace after the chaos?
- What tools or practices have helped you maintain your peace?
Reflect and journal your peace practices

Chapter 10: Dreaming Again

Reflection Prompt/Quiz:

- **What dreams have you reignited or discovered in your healing journey?**
- **What is your next step in pursuing those dreams?**
  Write your vision for the future

Chapter 11: Creating What I Dreamed

Reflection Prompt/Quiz:

- **What steps have you taken to turn your dreams into reality?**
- **What obstacles have you overcome, and how did you face them?**
  Reflect on your progress

Chapter 12: Lasting Impacts

Reflection Prompt/Quiz:

- How has your transformation impacted those around you?
- What legacy do you hope to leave?
  Journal your impact

Chapter 13: Embracing My Fullest Potential

Reflection Prompt/Quiz:

- What does embracing your fullest potential look like?
- How do you step into that power every day?
  Reflect and journal your next steps

Chapter 14: Living Authentically

Reflection Prompt/Quiz:

- How does living authentically change the way you engage with the world?
- What practices help you stay true to yourself?
  Write your thoughts

Conclusion: Embracing the Future

Reflection Prompt:

- Healing, rising, and reclaiming your power is a lifelong evolution. How do you see your future unfolding?
- What commitments are you making to yourself moving forward?
  Reflect and journal your promises

Acknowledgements

Reflection Prompt:

- Who supported you through your transformation?
- How can you honour your growth and those who helped you rise?
  Take a moment to express gratitude

About the Author

Reflection Prompt:

- **What part of your own story do you need to tell?**
- **What truth are you ready to claim?**
  Write your reflections

ACKNOWLEDGMENTS

To every woman who has ever chosen herself this book is for you.

Writing Phenomenal Women – Phoenix Rises was more than putting words on a page; it was reclaiming my voice. And while the journey was mine, I didn't walk it alone.

To my sisters, Mo, and Winnie thank you for being my anchor and my mirror. Your strength and unwavering support have held me through every storm.

To my warrior mother, Hermina your resilience runs through my veins. Thank you for your quiet power, your deep love, and the example you've always set.

In loving memory of my beautiful Sister Sharon, Natasha and Claudia three phenomenal women who walked beside me with grace, laughter, and boundless compassion. Your presence in my life was a gift, and your spirits continue to inspire me every day. This book carries pieces of all of you in every word.

To the women who shared their stories with me your courage helped me find mine. May we all continue to rise, again and again.

And finally, to the woman I used to be thank you for surviving, for choosing truth over comfort, and for never letting pain define you.

With deep gratitude and love,

Part I – The Fire

Chapter 1: The Illusion of Love

When I met him, I was drawn to his magnetism. He had a presence undeniable, electric. You felt seen, chosen, alive in his orbit. People gravitated toward him. And for a while, he made me feel like I was the centre of his universe.

But here's the truth about loving someone who is broken: You cannot love them whole. Not if they refuse to do the work themselves. And I didn't know it then, but I was pouring all my energy into someone who could never pour it back.

I saw the cracks early on. The subtle ways he pushed me aside for attention. How admiration from strangers seemed to feed him more than love from me.

Still, I believed I could be enough. I told myself, "Everyone has flaws. I can love him through this. I can show him what real love looks like."

What I didn't realise was that in doing so, I was slowly abandoning myself.

I let my boundaries slip. I silenced my needs. I told myself that patience was the answer. That one day he'd change. One day he'd recognise the depth of what we had. One day, he'd see me.

But someday never came.

Instead, I found myself performing emotional acrobatics constantly trying to hold everything together while shrinking parts of myself to make him feel whole.

At first, it was little things: The unexplained late nights. The white lies. The shallow conversations that skirted anything real. I told myself they were just bumps in the road. But deep down, I was ignoring the ache of truth: I was alone in the relationship.

I thought if I loved harder, waited longer, forgave more, he'd finally show up the way I needed him to. I thought if I held space for his pain, he'd eventually hold space for mine.

But the reality was brutal: I wasn't fixing anything. I was simply fading.

And the worst part? I knew it but I didn't want to admit it. Because admitting it meant accepting that my love wasn't enough to save us. Worse, it meant acknowledging that I hadn't been loving myself enough.

That was my deepest betrayal: not what he did to me but what I allowed to happen to me.

I gave someone the parts of me I should have been saving. And I did it in the name of love.

Chapter 1: The Illusion of Love (Continued)

The first few years were full of passion. The kind of fire that makes you feel alive like you're in the centre of something bigger than yourself. It felt like a dream. He was everything I thought I wanted.

He made me laugh. He made me feel seen in ways I hadn't before. I believed that's what love was those bright sparks of connection, the feeling of being chosen by someone who made you feel like the most important person in the room.

But over time, those sparks began to dim.

I started to notice things. He would disappear for hours at a time. And when he came back, there was always an excuse. I told myself it wasn't a big deal. After all, we were adults we

had our own lives, our work, our friends. Everyone needs space sometimes. I didn't want to seem insecure, needy, or jealous. So, I brushed it off.

Then came the lies.

At first, they were small harmless, I thought. Where were you last night? "Just out with the guys." What did you do? "Had a drink, hung out."

But something always felt off. His answers sounded rehearsed, too polished like he was performing sincerity. I kept telling myself, "It's fine. Let it go." But it wasn't fine. It never was. Because deep down, I knew. I knew the difference between truth and the things I was being fed. And I began to ask myself the one question that changes everything:

Am I really okay with this?

The first time I found out he was cheating, it wasn't explosive. It wasn't a confrontation or some messy discovery. It was quiet. A text message he forgot to delete. A name I didn't recognise. And suddenly, the pieces snapped into place. I wasn't crazy. My intuition had been right all along.

But I didn't scream. I didn't throw things. I didn't even ask him about it. I just sat there, staring at that screen, waiting for the wave to hit. And then it did but not with rage. With clarity.

Because in that moment, I understood something crucial: If I made a scene, I gave him power. He'd twist it. Blame me. Make me the problem. And I wasn't giving him that story.

I didn't need answers. I already knew. And the deeper truth that hit me was this: I had been clinging to a version of love that didn't exist. Not because he didn't care but because he was broken. And I couldn't fix broken. Not like that. Love was never supposed to be a repair project. It was meant to be mutual. Balanced. Safe.

And ours wasn't.

I was always the one giving, carrying, staying. He was always the one taking, escaping, searching for validation everywhere but with me.

Still, I stayed.

Not because I didn't know what was happening. But because I was afraid of what leaving meant. Leaving meant admitting I had poured years of love, effort, and belief into something that didn't love me back the way I deserved. It meant facing the shame of losing myself for someone who never saw my worth. I remember thinking, If I leave now, I'll never get that time back.

What I didn't see then was that time wasn't the thing I was losing. I was losing myself.

The next year was a slow fade. A quiet unravelling. There was no peace, only numbness. I numbed myself to his absences. To the lies. To the ache of feeling invisible.

I told myself: It's just a phase. He'll come around. He'll see what he has in me. I told myself to hold on, be patient, stay soft. But waiting for someone to change when they don't want to is like holding your breath forever.

And I couldn't breathe anymore.

I had stayed too long. For all the wrong reasons. Because admitting the truth would mean accepting that I had invested in a lie. But eventually, that truth became louder than the fear. And I couldn't ignore it anymore.

Because when you love someone more than you love yourself you don't just lose the relationship. You lose your reflection.

And I was finally ready to look in the mirror again.

Chapter 2: The Moment I Knew

I remember the exact moment I stopped pretending.

It wasn't dramatic.
It wasn't during a fight or an emotional outburst.
It was just me. Alone. Sitting in silence.

And for the first time, listening to my own truth.

I had been lying to myself for so long telling myself he'd change.
Telling myself he'd eventually see my worth.
That someday, he'd stop chasing validation from the outside world and finally look at what was right in front of him.

But something shifted in me that day.
A quiet, powerful knowing settled in:
This will never change.

He couldn't see me because he couldn't even see himself.
He was trying to fill a void I didn't create and I couldn't be the one to heal him.
No matter how deeply I loved, it was never going to be enough.

The more I stayed, the more I realised I wasn't just waiting for him to change.
I was waiting for my own permission to leave.

I had been holding out hope that one day I'd feel "ready,"
but that day doesn't come wrapped in clarity or closure.
It comes in silence.

And in that silence, I finally heard myself say:
Enough.

There was no yelling.
No drama.
No tears.

Just a quiet resolve.
I didn't need to be angry.
I didn't need him to apologise.
I didn't even need him to understand.

I just needed to choose *me*.

I had spent so long convincing myself that my loyalty would fix him.
That my softness would be enough to turn him into the man I believed he could be.

But that was the illusion I needed to let go of.
Because love doesn't require you to betray yourself.
It doesn't ask you to shrink.

That was the moment I realised:
I didn't need him to change I needed to change.
I needed to become the woman who no longer waited for someone else's permission to rise.

I wasn't afraid of losing him anymore.
I was afraid of continuing to lose *me*.

So, I started planning my exit.
Carefully. Quietly. With dignity.
No pleading. No revenge. No final speech.

I didn't need closure from him.
Because I had already given it to myself.

It was the most peaceful decision I've ever made.
And the most powerful.

Because the moment I chose myself
my soul finally exhaled.

And once I took that breath,
there was no turning back.

Chapter 3: Rising from the Ashes

The day I left wasn't marked by fireworks or fanfare. No one else would remember it but I always will. It was just me, standing quietly on the edge of something unknown, yet strangely familiar. It felt like stepping into the light after years of walking through shadows.

The first few days were surreal. Everything around me moved in slow motion. But I didn't cry. I didn't feel the anger or grief I thought would come. Instead, there was peace in the silence. For the first time in years, I could breathe without someone else's chaos filling the room. I could hear my own voice again.

And it was stronger than I remembered.

I didn't need anyone to validate my decision. I knew I'd done the right thing. The weight of his presence his needs, his drama, his emotional vacancy was gone. I had space. Space to think. To feel. To remember who I was before him.

The hardest part wasn't leaving him. The hardest part was rediscovering who I was without him.

For 18 years, my identity had been entangled with his moods, his needs, his shadows. Somewhere in that maze, I had lost sight of my own reflection. I had forgotten what made me laugh, what lit me up, what dreams were mine not shared, not borrowed, not buried.

So, I started small.

I reconnected with old friends. I took long walks. I lit candles for no reason and danced barefoot in my living room. I opened notebooks I hadn't touched in years, and I let myself feel the ache of abandoned passions.

And slowly, I began to rise.

But healing isn't a straight line. Some days, the doubt still crept in.

Loneliness would whisper in my ear, tempting me with the familiarity of dysfunction. I'd think, *Was it really that bad? Maybe I overreacted.* But then, I'd remember the lies. The betrayals. The nights I lay awake, aching for a version of him that didn't exist.

And I'd remember: **I left for a reason.**

I wasn't the same woman who once made herself small to make room for someone else's ego. I had outgrown that version of me. I was becoming someone new someone whole.

With every boundary I set, I reclaimed a part of myself. With every *no*, I said *yes* to me. I no longer needed to be anyone's saviour, anyone's emotional caretaker. I didn't need to fix the broken. I didn't need to earn love.

I already had love. Within me.

And then, as they always do, the past came knocking.

He reached out. At first, I ignored the messages. I didn't need his words. They no longer held power. But eventually, I answered. Not for closure. Not for validation. I answered because I had nothing to prove and nothing to hide.

He apologised. But it didn't move me. I had already forgiven him.

Not because he deserved it but because I did. I had forgiven myself first for staying too long, for silencing my intuition, for trying to fix what was never mine to mend.

And in that moment, I knew I had truly risen.

Chapter 4: The Expectation

At some point in those years, he stopped worrying about losing me. Somewhere between the broken promises and the quiet betrayals, he started to believe I would *always* be there. That no matter what he did, I'd stay. Because I always had.

In the beginning, I thought my loyalty was something he valued. I believed my willingness to stay through the storms, the silence, the scars was a reflection of strength. But what I thought was love… was actually control.

My devotion had become his insurance policy.

He knew I would forgive. He counted on it. He knew that after every lie, every betrayal, I'd pick up the pieces. I was the steady one. The safe place. The woman who'd always be there, waiting for him to be better.

And the worst part?

He was right.

I had taught him that my love was unconditional but not in the way love is meant to be. I had taught him that he could hurt me, and I would still stay. I had shown him that my needs didn't matter as much as his second chances.

Over time, I disappeared inside that pattern.

I stopped asking for more because I didn't want to be a burden. I stopped voicing my needs because I knew they wouldn't be met. And every time I gave more of myself, I lost a little more of who I was.

And he expected it.

He didn't change because he never had to. I was the constant. The caretaker. The forgiver. He wasn't afraid of losing me, because he thought I'd never leave.

But here's the truth:

Being expected is not the same as being valued.

The day that realisation hit me, something cracked open inside. I saw the relationship for what it was not a partnership, but a cycle. A loop where I kept hoping for something real, while he kept taking

what he never earned.

That's when I knew: staying wasn't love anymore. It was fear. Fear that I wouldn't find anything better. Fear that I wasn't enough on my own. Fear that walking away would mean admitting I had invested in the wrong person for far too long.

But I wasn't afraid anymore.

I left because I refused to be taken for granted one more day. I left because I deserved to be chosen not out of habit, but out of respect.

I wasn't going to keep showing up for someone who only noticed my absence when it threatened their comfort.

He expected me to be there.

And I chose not to be.

I chose to be somewhere I was seen. I chose to build a life that didn't depend on being someone's emotional crutch. I chose me not because he didn't choose me, but because *I finally did.*

Chapter 5: Learning to Trust Myself Again

After the dust settled, after the silence stopped feeling strange, I was left with something I hadn't expected: space. Not just in my home, or my schedule but in my mind. In my heart.

And at first, that space was terrifying.

For so long, I had filled every inch of my life with him his chaos, his needs, his moods. I knew how to survive in that space. I knew the rhythm of walking on eggshells, of making myself smaller so his shadows didn't stretch too far. But peace? Stillness? That was foreign territory.

And yet… that space held a promise.

It whispered, *you get to start over now.*

But starting over isn't just about new routines or clean slates. It's about rebuilding the things that were quietly dismantled piece by piece: your instincts, your confidence, your sense of worth. And for me, the hardest thing to rebuild was **trust in myself**.

Because the truth is, I didn't leave just because he hurt me. I left because I realised, I had stopped trusting *me*. I had ignored the voice inside me that had been whispering for years *this isn't right*. I had silenced my own knowing in the name of love, in the name of loyalty.

And that kind of self-betrayal takes time to heal.

So, I started small again.

I made tiny promises to myself and kept them. I'd say, *I'll go for a walk today*, and I did. *I'll drink water instead of wine tonight*, and I followed through. *I'll answer that call I've been avoiding. I'll write one honest sentence in my journal. I'll rest when I'm tired, even if the dishes aren't done.*

Each promise was a thread, weaving trust back into my bones.

And something unexpected happened.

As I rebuilt trust, I found myself craving less noise. Less validation.

Less distraction. I didn't need someone else to tell me I was doing the right thing I could feel it. My body knew. My breath deepened. My sleep softened. I stopped waiting for the other shoe to drop.

I stopped waiting for love to be painful in order to feel real.

And one day, I caught a glimpse of myself in the mirror not the tired version I'd grown used to, but someone steady. Someone soft and powerful. Someone who had walked through fire and didn't flinch at her reflection anymore.

That's when I realised:

Healing isn't about becoming someone new. It's about remembering who you were before the world told you to forget.

It's about returning to yourself. With love. With grace. With truth.

And no, I wasn't "fixed." I was never broken. I was just buried.

But I had finally started digging my way back.

Chapter 6: The Return of Joy

For a long time, I associated joy with guilt.

If I laughed too freely, I questioned it.

If I felt peace, I wondered how long it would last.

If something good happened, I braced for the crash.

I had spent years in a reality where joy was either performative or conditional something I had to earn by enduring enough pain, or something fleeting that I shouldn't get too attached to. And when I left, that belief didn't disappear overnight.

But slowly, joy found its way back in.

It came in unexpected ways quiet, ordinary, almost unremarkable moments.

The sun hitting my face during a morning walk.
A song from my childhood playing at the exact right time.
Laughing really laughing with a friend over something stupid and small.
Eating alone at a restaurant and realising I wasn't lonely. I was free.

These were not grand, sweeping moments of transformation. They were whispers. *Reminders that I was still alive. Still capable of feeling lightness. Still worthy of joy that didn't cost me pain first.*

And here's the thing no one tells you about healing:

Joy is a muscle.
If you've neglected it, it takes time to strengthen. You have to practice allowing it. At first, it feels awkward. Maybe even undeserved. But you keep showing up anyway. You let it in, even if it's just a flicker.

And with time, the flickers turn to flames.

I stopped needing a reason to feel good. I gave myself permission to enjoy things without needing to explain them. I stopped asking if I was allowed to feel happy. I stopped waiting for permission.

Because joy, I realised, wasn't something outside myself. It was something *within* me, waiting to be noticed again.

For so long, my story had been written in survival. In resilience. In grit. But I didn't want survival to be the whole story. I wanted softness. I wanted wonder. I wanted to stop bracing for impact and start leaning into the moment.

And eventually, I did.

Not because life got easier but because I stopped making joy the reward and started letting it be the reason.

The healing didn't erase the hurt, but it gave it context. It gave it contrast. And in that contrast, joy had room to breathe again.

Now, I don't just chase peace I protect it.
I don't just welcome joy I *honour* it.

Because I know what it cost to get here. And I'm not willing to shrink myself back into a life where joy is a luxury. Not when I've learned it's a right.

Chapter 7: Opening the Door Again

There came a time, quietly and without announcement, when I realised, I wasn't afraid anymore.

Not afraid of being alone.
Not afraid of the silence.
And maybe most surprising of all not afraid of being seen.

Because for years, I had lived behind a careful kind of armour. Smiling enough to seem okay. Nodding through conversations where I never really said much. Keeping my truth tucked safely beneath layers of "I'm fine."

But healing does something wild to you it invites you to open again.

Not recklessly. Not all at once. But piece by piece. A slow softening.

And so, I started letting people in.

At first, it was little things. Eye contact. Sitting still in moments of vulnerability without rushing to change the subject. Saying *how I really felt* when someone asked how I was not the polite version, but the honest one.

I started noticing who leaned in and who pulled away. Who saw me and who only saw what I could offer them. The difference was obvious now. I no longer confused attention with affection. I no longer mistook familiarity for safety.

And most of all, I no longer made excuses for anyone who made me feel small.

Because I wasn't small anymore. I wasn't shrinking to fit inside someone else's comfort zone. I had expanded and the people who were meant for me didn't flinch at my fullness.

I learned that boundaries weren't walls; they were invitations. Invitations to meet me where I was whole, healing, real. Not a version of me tailored to someone else's needs.

And slowly, I let a few people into that sacred space.

Not because I needed them to fix me *I was never broken*. But because connection, when chosen from a place of worth, feels different. Safer. Lighter. It isn't about proving your value. It's about sharing your presence.

I met people who didn't expect me to perform, who didn't shrink from my strength or edge away from my softness. I laughed more. Trusted more. Not everyone stayed but the ones who did, stayed fully.

And maybe, most importantly, I realized that I no longer feared intimacy.

Because I had finally become intimate with myself my truth, my story, my worth. I didn't need someone to complete me. I needed people who could meet me.

And now, I wait for no one to see my light before I believe it's there.

The door is open.
Not wide. But open.
And only those who come with respect, with presence, with clarity

they get to step inside.

Chapter 8: Redefining Love

For most of my life, love was something I survived.

It was a tightrope walk, a test, a proving ground. Something I had to earn by enduring. Something I held onto even when it hurt because I thought love meant holding on, no matter what.

I was taught that love was selfless. That it meant giving more, sacrificing more, staying longer. And I did. I gave until I was empty. I stayed until I disappeared. I believed that loving someone meant losing parts of myself along the way.

But I don't believe that anymore.

Because love real love doesn't require you to vanish.

It doesn't ask you to abandon yourself for someone else's comfort. It doesn't live in chaos. It doesn't thrive in silence or secrecy or sacrifice. Love isn't a battlefield. It's not a performance. It's not a reward you get for being "good enough."

Love is safe.
Love is steady.
Love sees you *all* of you and stays.

And before I could ever ask someone else to love me that way, I had to start with me.

So, I began redefining what love meant in my own life.

Love looked like boundaries that held.
Love looked like saying no without guilt.
Love looked like rest without shame, softness without apology, stillness without fear.

Love looked like protecting my peace even when no one understood why.

It wasn't glamorous. It wasn't loud. But it was mine.

And something powerful happened when I stopped chasing love and started *embodying* it.

I stopped feeling hungry for validation.
I stopped twisting myself into someone more palatable.
I stopped settling for half-hearted efforts and calling them connection.

Because now I knew what love wasn't and that made space for what it could be.

Love could be simple. Whole. Rooted in truth. Love could feel like home, not a hurricane. Love could expand me instead of exhausting me.

And maybe one day, someone will meet me in this version of love. Someone who doesn't flinch at my truth or shrink from my strength. Someone who brings their own fullness to the table not because they need to be completed, but because they want to *build*.

But I'm not waiting for that.

Because love already lives here. In the way I talk to myself. In the way I care for my body, tend to my heart, protect my energy. Love is in the way I've stopped abandoning myself for the comfort of others.

This is the love I wish I had known sooner.
But I'm grateful I know it now.

Because now, I don't just know what love is.

I know what I am not willing to call love ever again.

Chapter 9: Peace After the Storm

There's a moment in every storm when you realise the wind isn't the only thing shaking you. It's the weight of your own thoughts. The thundering noise of all the things you never said, all the things you were too afraid to face. The fear that what you're running from will follow you, that the storm is part of you and will never let go.

But what no one tells you is this:

The storm is not who you are. It is only what you've been through.

And eventually, the storm will pass. It always does.
And you'll be left with something quieter. Something deeper.
Something you can't see in the chaos, but you can feel as it settles.

Peace doesn't come from a perfect life.
It doesn't come from a smooth path, free of obstacles or pain.
It doesn't come from avoiding the things that scare you.

Peace comes from *choosing* to breathe.
Choosing to be still.

Choosing to trust that even in the mess, you are whole.

For a long time, I thought peace was something I had to fight for something that would arrive once all the pieces of my life were in place. But now I know:

Peace isn't a destination. It's a practice. A moment-by-moment decision to ground yourself, even when everything around you feels like it's moving too fast.

And here's the beauty of it:
You don't need to be perfect to have peace.
You don't need to have it all figured out.
You don't need to *earn* peace. It is already within you.

It took time for me to let go of the need to control, to be constantly on alert. To stop expecting the worst and start letting myself be *okay* even when I didn't have all the answers. I didn't have to fix everything, all the time.

And that shift letting go of the idea that I had to "fix" life was the quiet revolution.

I started saying no to the noise that didn't serve me.
I started honouring the silence in my life instead of filling it with distractions.
I gave myself permission to feel peace, even on days when I didn't feel happy, even when the world around me was chaotic.
Because peace isn't about perfect circumstances. It's about finding your centre in the midst of them.

In the quiet of my mornings, I learned to feel the weight of my own presence. I learned to listen to my body, to my breath, to my thoughts. I learned to sit in stillness without running from it.

I wasn't avoiding the storms anymore. I wasn't waiting for them to be gone before I could feel *safe*.

I was creating my own peace.
Within me.
Right now.

And the more I practiced that peace, the more it filled every part of my life. The decisions became clearer. My relationships became lighter. I became less afraid of the future and more grateful for the present.

Because peace is never about what's coming or what's already passed. Peace is the space where you stand, in this moment, with all that you are.

And I was learning to stand in my own light.
To be my own calm.
To create a peace that no one could take from me.

Chapter 10: Dreaming Again

For so long, I was afraid to dream.

Not because I didn't want a better future, but because I had convinced myself that dreaming was for people who hadn't been through the storm. People who hadn't tasted pain, loss, or disappointment. I thought that to dream was to invite disappointment. That hope would only let me down.

But what I realised, after all this time, was that dreaming isn't about *waiting* for things to be perfect. It's about daring to believe in *possibilities* again even when the road ahead isn't clear, and even when the past still lingers like a shadow.

I started small.

It wasn't about designing a grand vision of my life all at once it was about allowing myself the space to desire *anything* at all. It was about thinking beyond survival and considering what *joy* could look like, what *expansion* could feel like, and what freedom meant.

I began asking myself:

What does my soul crave?
What kind of life do I want to create for myself just for me?
What would it feel like to be free of the weight of the past?

And for the first time in years, I allowed myself to answer. Not from a place of neediness or desperation, but from a place of *wholeness*. I didn't need to dream from a place of lack. I dreamed from a place of abundance, abundance of wisdom, strength, and love. The kind that doesn't need to prove anything to anyone.

So, I let myself dream of things I had put aside:
A small house by the sea.
Travelling to places I'd always longed to visit.
Writing stories that came from my heart.
Learning how to paint, just because it made me feel alive.
Falling in love with a life that didn't ask me to shrink.

The thing about dreams, when they're born from this place of peace, is that they don't come with urgency. There's no pressure to make them happen *right now*. It's not about rushing. It's about *nurturing* them. Letting them unfold on their own time, with patience and grace.

I learned that dreaming is not about perfection it's about direction. It's about saying: *Yes, I am worthy of more. Yes, I deserve the life I envision, just because I exist.*

I no longer measured myself by how much I had or how far I'd come. I measured myself by how much I could *imagine*, by how deeply I could *trust* that my dreams were already unfolding. Because I knew now, more than ever, that the universe moves in mysterious ways, and I am part of that dance.

I began building a life around the idea that joy doesn't have to be earned, that love doesn't have to be sacrificed, that peace doesn't have to be fleeting.

I didn't just dream about what I wanted I started making it real, piece by piece. I gave myself permission to want big things again. To believe that the best was yet to come. And most importantly, I learned to be *okay* with not knowing exactly how it would all unfold.

Because the truth is, I'll never have all the answers. But I know enough now to trust that each step I take will lead me closer to a future I can't yet fully imagine.

And that's the beauty of dreaming again.

You don't have to know the destination, but you can trust that the journey is already worth it.

Chapter 11: Creating What I Dreamed

For so long, I'd been a passenger in my own life.
Watching as time passed, letting things happen to me instead of

making them happen. I told myself it was fate. I told myself I had no control. But deep down, I knew I had simply stopped believing that I could shape my own reality.

I had been waiting for permission, for the right moment, for the stars to align.

But I learned something powerful:

I am the one who gets to decide when the moment is right.
I am the one who gets to decide when the stars align.

So, I stopped waiting.

The first step wasn't as dramatic as I thought it would be. It wasn't a huge leap. It was simply showing up every day, with intention. Showing up for my dreams, for my future, for the version of me I had yet to become. I started treating my desires with respect not as distant hopes, but as seeds I was ready to plant and nurture.

I started saying *yes* to the things that scared me, that excited me, that made me feel alive.
I started showing up for myself, even when the path wasn't clear.
I stopped doubting and started *doing*.

Because the truth is, nothing happens unless you *act*. Nothing shifts until you move.

I took the first step, then the second. And before I knew it, the momentum was building. Each small step felt like a victory. Each effort, no matter how small, began to create the life I had dreamed of one decision at a time.

I started writing more.
I started planning trips I had once thought impossible.

I began taking up space in the world, in conversations, in rooms I once thought were out of my reach.
I found new passions. I embraced old ones. I created a life that reflected my worth, my dreams, and my own deep love for the journey ahead.

It wasn't always easy. Sometimes, the old fears would creep in. The voices that told me I wasn't enough, that I wasn't capable, that I didn't deserve this.

But now, I had something stronger than fear: *conviction*.

I had already walked through the storm. I had already rebuilt. And now I had a deep knowing that I could handle whatever came next.

So, I kept moving.
Kept creating.
Kept believing.

Because here's the secret:

The life I dreamed of was always mine to create. I just had to give myself permission to live it.

And now, I am. Every single day.

Chapter 12: Lasting Impacts

The changes weren't always dramatic. They didn't always feel like fireworks or grand declarations. But they were there, shifting in the quiet spaces of my life. The real work the work that truly transformed me wasn't the big moments, but the small, everyday choices. The ways I started showing up for myself, the boundaries I set, the clarity with which I spoke my truth.

And slowly, the people around me started noticing.

Some of them, who had always expected me to shrink, began to feel uncomfortable with my growth. They didn't know how to handle this new version of me. They didn't know how to interact with a woman who no longer dimmed her light to make them feel better. They didn't know what to do with someone who stopped apologising for her needs.

But here's the thing:

I no longer needed their approval.

For the first time, I didn't seek validation from others. I didn't need to be anyone's emotional caretaker. I didn't need to fill the gaps of someone else's brokenness. I was no longer available to be anyone's excuse for staying small.

And that's when I realised how deep the transformation had really gone.

I began noticing how my relationships had shifted how the dynamics had changed, sometimes in ways that were uncomfortable, sometimes in ways that were liberating.

Some people drifted away, naturally. I wasn't the version of myself they had become accustomed to, and without that familiarity, there was no longer space for them in my life. It wasn't about rejection. It was just that we no longer fit.

But there were also those who stayed. Those who embraced my

growth, who celebrated my evolution, who saw the changes and chose to support them. These relationships were different stronger, more authentic. There was no longer a need to *perform* or pretend. We could just be. And in that, we became more.

The most profound shift, however, was in how I saw *myself*.

The version of me that had once been so eager to sacrifice, to give, to keep everyone around her comfortable she was gone. And in her place stood a woman who was unapologetically herself. Who knew her worth. Who wasn't afraid to ask for what she needed. Who trusted that her voice mattered.

For so long, I had believed that I wasn't enough on my own. That I needed to be chosen, to be validated, to be *needed*. But I learned that the most lasting impact of all was this:

I *chose* myself.

And because of that, I could now show up fully for the people who mattered. I could be present. I could love with a heart that wasn't tethered to past wounds or self-doubt. I could give freely without the need to "earn" love or approval.

I wasn't afraid of what I might lose anymore. I wasn't afraid of being misunderstood. I wasn't afraid of the future.

Because the truth was, I had already found everything I needed within myself. I had already created the life I dreamed of.

And now, I could let go of the past and embrace a future where everything I wanted was already on its way.

Chapter 13: Embracing My Fullest Potential

For so long, I had been playing small. Not because I didn't have the potential, but because I didn't believe I was worthy of the life I truly wanted. I didn't believe that someone like me someone who had been through so much deserved to rise any higher.

But now, as I stood at the edge of this new chapter, I saw something different:

The sky was not the limit.
I was the limit.

The truth is, we often limit ourselves by the stories we tell. The ones that say we're not good enough, not capable enough, not worthy enough. The ones that make us believe our past defines our future. But what I've come to realise is that every story can be rewritten. Every belief can be challenged. And every boundary can be expanded.

I wasn't just *healing*. I was *growing*.

And growth doesn't stop. It's a constant evolution. It's the courage to face the unknown and the faith to trust that you can handle whatever comes next.

For the first time in my life, I wasn't afraid of what lay ahead. I wasn't terrified of the unknown or unsure about what I was capable of. I didn't need to be perfect. I didn't need to have it all figured out.

I simply needed to keep moving forward, trusting that I was always capable of more than I believed.

There were still challenges, of course. There were days when the doubts tried to creep in, when fear whispered that maybe I wasn't as strong as I thought. But now, when those voices appeared, I didn't listen. I simply acknowledged them and let them pass, knowing that they didn't define me anymore.

I had learned that embracing my potential wasn't about waiting for a magical moment or for someone else to give me permission. It was about making the decision to believe in myself, even when the world around me didn't.

So, I began stepping into spaces I once thought I wasn't ready for. I began taking risks, pushing myself beyond the boundaries I had set, and discovering just how limitless I could be.

I took on challenges I once would have turned away from.
I spoke my truth without fear of rejection.
I gave myself permission to grow beyond the woman I was yesterday, beyond the dreams I once thought too big.

And with each new step, I realised that the journey is not just about reaching a destination. It's about *who you become* along the way. It's about learning to embrace your full power, to walk with courage, and to trust that every part of you every scar, every strength, every lesson has brought you to this moment of possibility.

Because here's the truth I now know:

There is no limit to what I can create. There is no ceiling to my potential.
I can continue to rise, continue to expand, and continue to evolve. And I will.

The future is not a place to fear. It is a place to embrace.

Because now, I know that I am *worthy* of it all.

Chapter 14: Living Authentically

For the first time in my life, I wasn't trying to fit into someone else's version of who I should be. I wasn't bending or shaping myself to meet the expectations of others. I wasn't silencing parts of myself or dimming my light to make other people comfortable.

I was simply *me* whole, unapologetic, and at peace with every part of who I was.

Living authentically isn't about being perfect. It's not about having all the answers or presenting a flawless version of yourself to the world. It's about being honest with yourself and the people around you, about embracing both the light and the shadows within you.

And it's liberating.

I no longer felt the need to seek approval, validation, or acceptance from others. I didn't need anyone to tell me I was enough, because I knew that I was. I didn't need to explain my choices or justify my boundaries. I didn't need to apologise for wanting more, for speaking my truth, for taking up space in the world.

Living authentically is about trusting that who you are is enough. It's about knowing that you have value, regardless of what anyone else thinks. That your worth isn't tied to your achievements, your relationships, or your past mistakes. It's simply intrinsic.

And as I embraced this truth, I noticed something incredible: the people who were meant to be in my life showed up. I wasn't trying to fit into any mould, and yet, the relationships that came into my world felt deep, genuine, and unforced. The love I attracted wasn't based on who I *pretended* to be, but on who I truly was.

I found myself surrounded by people who celebrated my authenticity, who supported me without trying to change me, and who encouraged me to keep evolving. These were the connections I had been searching for all along not the ones based on obligation or performance, but the ones based on real, raw, unfiltered love.

Living authentically also meant letting go of the need to control every outcome. I learned to stop worrying about how things would unfold and instead trust that everything was happening exactly as it should. I stopped fearing rejection, because I realised that when you live authentically, you attract the right people and the right opportunities.

I allowed myself to make mistakes and embrace imperfection. I forgave myself for the times I had fallen short and celebrated the ways I had grown. Every moment, every lesson, every setback became a part of the tapestry of who I was. And with each passing day, I felt more *alive* in my own skin.

Living authentically meant I no longer had to fight to be seen.
I was already seen by myself.
And that was enough.

The world may not always understand you. People may not always agree with your choices. But when you live authentically, you no longer need their approval. You are free from the weight of trying to be something you're not. And that freedom is priceless.

Because when you live authentically, you are finally *home*.

And there is no place more powerful, more peaceful, and more true than that.

ABOUT THE AUTHOR

Donn C. McCalla - lives a quiet, grounded life centred around love, faith, and family. She doesn't seek attention or validation through social media. Instead, she chooses peace, presence, and purpose living authentically, loving deeply, and nurturing those around her.

After walking away from nearly two decades in a relationship marked by betrayal and emotional absence, she rose not in rage, but in quiet strength. Her story is one of truth, self-respect, and the kind of grace that doesn't need an audience.

Phenomenal Women - **"How I Lost Myself – And Found the Fire to Rise Again"**

is her first book a heartfelt offering to every woman who stayed too long, gave too much, and is finally ready to come home to herself.

She writes not for recognition, but for healing. Not to be seen, but to be heard.

Not to relive the pain, but to rise from it.

With love and faith,

Donn C. McCalla

Phenomenal Women - "How I Lost Myself – And Found the Fire to Rise Again"

A woman doesn't always rise in fire.

Sometimes, she rises in silence

with clarity, with grace, and without apology.

After nearly two decades in a relationship marked by betrayal, emotional neglect, and quiet suffering, Donn walked away. Not in chaos, not in anger but in peace. Her strength wasn't loud. It didn't need to be.

This is her story.

A raw, honest, and deeply empowering journey through love, loss, healing, and rebirth. A tribute to every woman who stayed too long, gave too much, and finally found the courage to choose herself.

This is not a tale of bitterness.

It's a testimony of self-respect.

A reclamation of identity.

A rising from the ashes with grace.

Phenomenal Women - "How I Lost Myself – And Found the Fire

to Rise Again"

is more than a book. It's a reminder:

You are allowed to leave.

You are allowed to heal.

And you are allowed to rise.

Reflection on the Full Manuscript

The manuscript starts with a **quiet departure** the moment of leaving behind a toxic relationship that had defined the narrator's life for years. In **Chapter 3**, the protagonist begins to rediscover themselves after stepping away from the chaos and emotional weight of the past. The initial peace and self-reflection are felt deeply, but the real struggle is not just the physical act of leaving it's the emotional and psychological process of rediscovering who they are without the influence of the relationship. This chapter sets the tone for the journey ahead: that healing is not linear but is deeply personal and ongoing.

In **Chapter 4**, the narrator examines the unhealthy dynamics of the past relationship, realising how they had allowed themselves to become *expected* always there to forgive, always there to provide emotional support. This chapter uncovers the truth that **love without self-worth is not love**; it's sacrifice, and that sacrifice comes at the cost of one's identity. The insight gained here *being expected is not the same as being valued* is a pivotal realisation. It's an awakening to the fact that real love requires mutual respect, not a one-sided commitment.

As the manuscript progresses, we witness the narrator's **emotional reclamation**. In **Chapter 5**, they begin to realise their own needs and start setting boundaries. This chapter explores the **power of**

saying "no" a simple word that becomes a powerful tool of self-preservation. Each boundary set is an act of self-love and respect. This transformation isn't without doubt, as the narrator faces the temptation of returning to old patterns, but their newfound strength keeps them from looking back.

By **Chapter 11**, the narrator begins to **actively create the life they dreamed of**. They stop waiting for external validation and take ownership of their future. This chapter marks the shift from passive longing to active creation. It's a defining moment where dreams no longer feel distant or impossible they are something within reach, something the narrator is now actively shaping. This is where they start to show up for themselves, without hesitation or apology.

In **Chapter 12**, the lasting impacts of the narrator's transformation become clear. **Relationships shift**, as some people fall away while others step in to support this new, empowered version of the protagonist. This chapter delves into how **authenticity** and growth naturally create the space for the right people to enter one's life, while those who are threatened by change fade into the background. It's a quiet realisation that not everyone will walk with you on this journey, but those who remain will do so because they truly see you.

By **Chapter 13**, the narrator embraces their **full potential** stepping beyond the limitations they once placed on themselves. They stop fearing the unknown and start living with a sense of boundless possibility. It's the moment when they realise that the only limit they have is the one they set for themselves. This is the true power of transformation: to move forward with courage and trust in the face of uncertainty.

Finally, **Chapter 14** brings the story full circle, embracing the power of **living authentically**. This chapter is about the peace that comes when you no longer seek approval from others. The narrator fully accepts their worth and their identity, no longer afraid to show up as their true self. This is the ultimate freedom the freedom to be who you truly are, without apology. The relationships that form as a result of this authenticity are real and nourishing. The narrator realises that **living authentically means being at peace with yourself**, and that peace is the foundation for everything else in life.

Key Themes and Takeaways

1. **Self-Worth and Authenticity**: The central theme of the manuscript is the journey to self-discovery and the realisation that self-worth is not something that should be sacrificed in relationships or for others. The narrator learns that true love is rooted in mutual respect, and that the most powerful love of all is self-love.
2. **Empowerment through Boundaries**: A significant shift occurs when the narrator begins setting boundaries. This isn't just about saying "no" it's about reclaiming agency, protecting one's emotional health, and learning to prioritise oneself. This marks the point where the protagonist steps into their power.
3. **Transformation as a Continuous Journey**: The manuscript makes it clear that personal transformation doesn't happen overnight. It's a process of small, consistent actions, shifts in perspective, and learning to let go of old patterns. Healing is a journey, but the protagonist learns that each step forward is worth celebrating.
4. **The Courage to Change**: The narrator's courage to change, to walk away from what no longer serves them, is a recurring theme. Every chapter brings a new moment of strength, and it's clear that courage isn't the absence of fear, but the decision to move forward despite it.

5. **Freedom in Self-Acceptance**: The final chapters underscore the peace and power that come from living authentically. The narrator stops seeking approval and starts embracing their true self, which in turn invites more genuine relationships and opportunities.

Overall Reflection

This manuscript is a powerful narrative about **rediscovery, healing, and personal growth**. It offers readers an inspiring look at what it means to reclaim one's life, identity, and self-worth after experiencing emotional hardship. It speaks to the universal experience of finding strength in vulnerability, of learning to say "no" and reclaim one's voice, and of stepping into a life that reflects the deepest truth of who you are.

The journey is not easy, and it's not always linear but it is *worth it*. By the end of this manuscript, the protagonist has fully embraced their potential, learned to love themselves, and begun living in alignment with their authentic truth. This story is an empowering reminder that **we have the power to create our own reality** and that the greatest love story we will ever have is the one we build with ourselves.

Quiz 1: Are You Living Authentically?

This quiz helps readers explore whether they are fully embracing their true selves or if they are still hiding parts of who they are.

1. **When I make decisions, I consider:**

- a) What others will think or how they will react.
- b) What feels true and right for me, regardless of others' opinions.
- c) What will make the people around me happy or comfortable.

2. **I feel comfortable setting boundaries in relationships:**
   - a) Rarely I feel guilty or anxious when I say "no."
   - b) Sometimes I'm still learning how to say "no" without feeling bad.
   - c) Most of the time I'm confident in expressing my limits.

3. **How often do you feel like you're pretending to be someone you're not?**
   - a) Almost all the time.
   - b) Occasionally, but I'm trying to stop.
   - c) Rarely, I'm generally comfortable with who I am.

4. **When it comes to my dreams and goals, I:**
   - a) Often push them aside because I don't believe I deserve them.
   - b) Sometimes pursue them but hold back out of fear of judgment.
   - c) Actively work toward them, trusting that they are mine to claim.

5. **How do you feel about your imperfections?**
   - a) I try to hide them, as I fear being judged.
   - b) I accept them, but sometimes I still struggle with self-criticism.
   - c) I embrace them as part of who I am, knowing they make me unique.

Results:

- Mostly **A's**: You might still be struggling with authenticity. It could be helpful to take time to reflect on what truly matters to you and start practicing self-acceptance.

- Mostly **B's**: You're on the right path! You're learning to embrace your authentic self, but there's still work to be done in letting go of fear and self-doubt.
- Mostly **C's**: You are living authentically and embracing your true self. Keep trusting your intuition and continue walking in your truth!

Quiz 2: Are You Honouring Your Self-Worth?

This quiz helps readers reflect on whether they're truly valuing themselves and their needs.

1. **How often do you feel that you deserve happiness and success?**
    - a) Rarely sometimes I feel unworthy of the good things in life.
    - b) Sometimes I'm learning to believe in my worth more.
    - c) Most of the time I know I deserve happiness and success.
2. **When someone asks for your help, you:**
    - a) Often feel obligated to say yes, even when you don't have the energy or desire.
    - b) Consider it but feel conflicted about putting your needs aside.
    - c) Assess if it aligns with your values and priorities before agreeing.
3. **Do you forgive yourself easily when you make a mistake?**
    - a) No, I tend to be hard on myself and hold onto guilt.

- o b) Sometimes, but I still struggle with self-criticism.
- o c) Yes, I recognise that mistakes are part of growth and learn from them.

4. **In your relationships, do you feel respected and valued?**
    - o a) Not always I often feel taken for granted or unnoticed.
    - o b) Sometimes I'm still learning to set boundaries and ask for what I need.
    - o c) Yes, I'm surrounded by people who appreciate me for who I truly am.

5. **When you experience success or a compliment, you:**
    - o a) Brush it off or downplay it, feeling undeserving.
    - o b) Appreciate it but feel a little uncomfortable accepting praise.
    - o c) Fully accept and celebrate it, knowing it's well-earned.

Results:

- Mostly **A's**: It's time to start focusing on your self-worth. You deserve happiness, success, and respect practice self-compassion and affirm your value daily.
- Mostly **B's**: You're beginning to recognize your worth, but there's still room to grow. Consider ways you can prioritise your needs and practice self-love.
- Mostly **C's**: You're honouring your self-worth and embracing your value. Keep nurturing this mindset and continue to surround yourself with people who respect and appreciate you.

Quiz 3: Are You Ready to Embrace Your Full Potential?

This quiz helps readers assess how ready they are to fully step into their greatness and pursue their dreams.

1. **When you think about your goals, you:**
    - a) Feel overwhelmed and unsure if you can achieve them.
    - b) Have a few doubts, but you try to take small steps forward.
    - c) Feel excited and motivated to pursue them, knowing you're capable.
2. **How comfortable are you with taking risks?**
    - a) Not comfortable I prefer to stay in my comfort zone.
    - b) Somewhat comfortable I'm starting to push myself out of my comfort zone.
    - c) Very comfortable I embrace risks as opportunities to grow.
3. **Do you trust that you have the strength to handle challenges?**
    - a) Not always I often doubt myself when challenges arise.
    - b) Sometimes I'm still working on building my confidence.
    - c) Yes, I trust that I am resilient and can handle whatever comes my way.
4. **How often do you take time for personal growth and reflection?**
    - a) Rarely I often get caught up in the busyness of life.
    - b) Occasionally I try to reflect, but it's not always consistent.
    - c) Regularly I make time for growth, reflection, and self-improvement.

5. **When you think about your future, you:**
    - a) Feel uncertain or fearful about what lies ahead.
    - b) Have some worries, but I believe things will work out in the end.
    - c) Feel hopeful and excited for all the possibilities ahead.

Results:

- Mostly **A's**: You may still have doubts about your potential. It's time to start trusting in yourself and taking small steps toward your goals. You are capable of more than you realize!
- Mostly **B's**: You're on the right track! Embrace the uncertainty, take risks, and believe in your ability to handle whatever comes your way.
- Mostly **C's**: You are ready to step into your full potential. Keep moving forward with confidence and excitement and continue to pursue your dreams with courage and clarity.

Reflective Workbook: Embracing Your Journey of Transformation

Introduction

Congratulations on completing the manuscript! Now, it's time to turn inward and reflect on your own journey. This workbook is designed to help you take the lessons and insights from the book and apply them to your life. Each quiz encourages you to explore your authenticity, self-worth, and potential. Take your time with each section and be gentle with yourself this is your journey.

Quiz 1: Are You Living Authentically?

Reflect on how you're showing up in the world. Are you being true to yourself, or are there parts of you still hidden?

1. **When I make decisions, I consider:**
    - a) What others will think or how they will react.
    - b) What feels true and right for me, regardless of others' opinions.
    - c) What will make the people around me happy or comfortable.
2. **I feel comfortable setting boundaries in relationships:**
    - a) Rarely I feel guilty or anxious when I say "no."
    - b) Sometimes I'm still learning how to say "no" without feeling bad.
    - c) Most of the time I'm confident in expressing my limits.
3. **How often do you feel like you're pretending to be someone you're not?**
    - a) Almost all the time.
    - b) Occasionally, but I'm trying to stop.
    - c) Rarely, I'm generally comfortable with who I am.
4. **When it comes to my dreams and goals, I:**
    - a) Often push them aside because I don't believe I deserve them.
    - b) Sometimes pursue them but hold back out of fear of judgment.

- c) Actively work toward them, trusting that they are mine to claim.
5. **How do you feel about your imperfections?**
    - a) I try to hide them, as I fear being judged.
    - b) I accept them, but sometimes I still struggle with self-criticism.
    - c) I embrace them as part of who I am, knowing they make me unique.

Results:

- Mostly **A's**: You may still be struggling with authenticity. Consider taking time to reflect on what truly matters to you and start practicing self-acceptance.
- Mostly **B's**: You're on the right path! You're learning to embrace your authentic self, but there's still work to be done in letting go of fear and self-doubt.
- Mostly **C's**: You are living authentically and embracing your true self. Keep trusting your intuition and continue walking in your truth!

Quiz 2: Are You Honouring Your Self-Worth?

Reflect on whether you are valuing yourself in the way you deserve. Are you practicing self-love and setting healthy boundaries?

1. **How often do you feel that you deserve happiness and success?**
    - a) Rarely sometimes I feel unworthy of the good things in life.
    - b) Sometimes I'm learning to believe in my worth more.
    - c) Most of the time I know I deserve happiness and success.
2. **When someone asks for your help, you:**
    - a) Often feel obligated to say yes, even when you don't have the energy or desire.
    - b) Consider it but feel conflicted about putting your needs aside.
    - c) Assess if it aligns with your values and priorities before agreeing.
3. **Do you forgive yourself easily when you make a mistake?**
    - a) No, I tend to be hard on myself and hold onto guilt.
    - b) Sometimes, but I still struggle with self-criticism.
    - c) Yes, I recognize that mistakes are part of growth and learn from them.
4. **In your relationships, do you feel respected and valued?**
    - a) Not always I often feel taken for granted or unnoticed.
    - b) Sometimes I'm still learning to set boundaries and ask for what I need.
    - c) Yes, I'm surrounded by people who appreciate me for who I truly am.
5. **When you experience success or a compliment, you:**
    - a) Brush it off or downplay it, feeling undeserving.
    - b) Appreciate it but feel a little uncomfortable accepting praise.
    - c) Fully accept and celebrate it, knowing it's well-earned.

Results:

- Mostly **A's**: It's time to start focusing on your self-worth. You deserve happiness, success, and respect practice self-compassion and affirm your value daily.
- Mostly **B's**: You're beginning to recognize your worth, but there's still room to grow. Consider ways you can prioritise your needs and practice self-love.
- Mostly **C's**: You're honouring your self-worth and embracing your value. Keep nurturing this mindset and continue to surround yourself with people who respect and appreciate you.

Quiz 3: Are You Ready to Embrace Your Full Potential?

Reflect on whether you're truly stepping into your greatness. Are you ready to pursue your dreams and embrace the life you deserve?

1. **When you think about your goals, you:**
    - a) Feel overwhelmed and unsure if you can achieve them.
    - b) Have a few doubts, but you try to take small steps forward.
    - c) Feel excited and motivated to pursue them, knowing you're capable.
2. **How comfortable are you with taking risks?**
    - a) Not comfortable I prefer to stay in my comfort zone.
    - b) Somewhat comfortable I'm starting to push myself out of my comfort zone.

- c) Very comfortable I embrace risks as opportunities to grow.

3. **Do you trust that you have the strength to handle challenges?**
    - a) Not always I often doubt myself when challenges arise.
    - b) Sometimes I'm still working on building my confidence.
    - c) Yes, I trust that I am resilient and can handle whatever comes my way.

4. **How often do you take time for personal growth and reflection?**
    - a) Rarely I often get caught up in the busyness of life.
    - b) Occasionally I try to reflect, but it's not always consistent.
    - c) Regularly I make time for growth, reflection, and self-improvement.

5. **When you think about your future, you:**
    - a) Feel uncertain or fearful about what lies ahead.
    - b) Have some worries, but I believe things will work out in the end.
    - c) Feel hopeful and excited for all the possibilities ahead.

Results:

- Mostly **A's**: You may still have doubts about your potential. It's time to start trusting in yourself and taking small steps toward your goals. You are capable of more than you realize!
- Mostly **B's**: You're on the right track! Embrace the uncertainty, take risks, and believe in your ability to handle whatever comes your way.
- Mostly **C's**: You are ready to step into your full potential. Keep moving forward with confidence and excitement and continue to pursue your dreams with courage and clarity.

Conclusion: Your Path Forward

Congratulations on completing this workbook! Reflect on your results and take note of any areas where you'd like to grow. Transformation is an ongoing process, and now that you've taken the time to assess where you stand, you have a clearer idea of the next steps in your journey.

Take Action:

- Identify one area where you'd like to make a change and set an intention for growth.
- Journal about your experience throughout this workbook. What did you learn about yourself? What shifts can you begin making today?
- Celebrate your progress whether big or small. Every step you take toward living authentically and honouring your self-worth is worth acknowledging.

Additional Resources:

- *Recommended Reading*: Books, pod casts, or articles on personal growth, authenticity, and self-love.
- *Action Plan*: A space for the reader to write out specific actions they'll take based on their quiz results.

---

1. Journaling Prompts

Journaling is a powerful tool for reflection and adding a few specific prompts throughout the workbook can encourage readers to dive deeper into their emotions, experiences, and insights.

- **Example Journal Prompts**:
  - *What are the three biggest obstacles you've faced in standing in your truth? How did they affect your sense of self-worth?*
  - *Reflect on a time when you were your most authentic self. How did that feel, and how can you bring more of that into your daily life?*
  - *Think about a moment when you put someone else's needs above your own. How did that impact your mental and emotional well-being?*

2. Action Plan Pages

After each quiz or reflection section, offer an "Action Plan" for readers to jot down tangible steps they can take to apply the lessons learned from the quizzes. These action steps could include setting specific goals or journaling exercises to solidify the changes they wish to make in their life.

Action Plan Example:

- What did I learn from this section?
- What is one action I will take today to honour my self-worth/authenticity/potential?
- Who can I turn to for support as I make these changes?

Giving readers a **concrete next step** makes the workbook feel more like a **living, actionable guide** rather than just a reflective tool.

3. Affirmations

Positive affirmations can be a helpful tool for readers who are working on improving their mindset and self-worth. You could sprinkle affirmations throughout the workbook that are in line with each section's theme (authenticity, self-worth, potential).

Examples:

- "I am worthy of love, respect, and all the good things life has to offer."
- "I trust myself and my intuition to guide me on the path of my true purpose."
- "I honour my needs and make space for what truly serves my growth."

Encourage readers to write their own personalized affirmations as well. This can be done as part of the action plan.

4. Worksheets or Exercises

Consider adding **worksheets or mini exercises** throughout the workbook that encourage readers to go beyond introspection and into action. For example:

- **Vision Board Exercise**: Guide readers to create a vision for their future self. What does their life look like when they fully embrace their authenticity, self-worth, and potential? Have them sketch or write out their vision and set a few actionable steps to move toward it.
- **Goal-Setting Worksheet**: Break down larger goals into actionable steps and help them track progress over time.

5. Quotes and Inspiration

Adding **inspirational quotes** throughout the workbook can serve as motivation for readers. This can act as a reminder that transformation is a process, and they are not alone in their journey.

Examples:

- "You are not a product of your circumstances. You are a product of your decisions." - Stephen R. Covey
- "The most courageous act is still to think for yourself. Aloud." - Coco Chanel
- "Your value doesn't decrease based on someone's inability to see your worth." - Unknown

6. Interactive Checkpoints

After every few pages or sections, you could include a **"checkpoint"** that encourages readers to pause and assess their emotional state or progress.

Example:

- "How do you feel right now? Check in with yourself. Are you noticing any shifts or resistance as you work through this section? Take a deep breath, and jot down whatever comes to mind."

This helps readers keep track of their emotions and growth as they move through the workbook, offering them a moment to recalibrate and reengage if needed.

7. Accountability Partner or Group

While this workbook can be a solo journey, having **accountability** can enhance its impact. Encourage readers to consider sharing parts of their workbook with a trusted friend, family member, or even a support group. This could be a great way to build community and encourage deeper exploration.

Example:

- "Consider sharing one of your journal entries or action plans with an accountability partner who can offer feedback and support."

In Summary:

Your workbook is already on a strong path, but here are the **additional features** I suggest to enrich the experience:

1. **Journaling Prompts**: Encourage deeper reflection and emotional processing.

2. **Action Plan Pages**: Make the workbook actionable by setting specific next steps.
3. **Affirmations**: Offer a tool to change mindset and build self-worth.
4. **Worksheets/Exercises**: Provide activities that help readers integrate the material.
5. **Inspirational Quotes**: Keep the energy high with motivational words.
6. **Interactive Checkpoints**: Remind readers to pause, reflect, and recalibrate.
7. **Accountability Partner/Group**: Invite readers to share their journey with someone for support.

Let's break this down and create those elements in more detail, step by step, so we can really enhance the workbook and give your readers a holistic, actionable experience.

1. Journaling Prompts

These prompts will help your readers dive deep into their personal reflections and understand where they stand in their journey of transformation. Here's a more robust list of prompts to include:

Section: Authenticity

- *Think about a recent decision you made. Were you being true to yourself, or did you make the decision to please others? Write about how that felt.*
- *What does being authentic mean to you? What does it look like in your everyday life? Write a description of your "authentic self."*

- *When was the last time you felt proud of yourself for showing up as your true self? Describe the situation and the emotions it stirred in you.*
- *Reflect on a time when you hid parts of yourself to avoid conflict or rejection. What was the result? How would you handle it differently now?*

Section: Self-Worth

- *Think about a time when you accepted less than you deserved from someone. What could you have done differently to honour your self-worth in that situation?*
- *What are three things that make you feel worthy of love and respect? Write them down and reflect on how you can remind yourself of them daily.*
- *When you are in a tough situation, do you give yourself grace? Write about how you show compassion to yourself during challenging times.*
- *List three ways you've seen yourself grow in terms of valuing yourself over the past year. How have you changed?*

Section: Embracing Potential

- *What is one goal that you have put off because of fear or doubt? Why have you avoided it, and how can you take a small step toward it today?*
- *When you think about your future, what excites you most? What holds you back from fully stepping into that future?*
- *Think about a time when you overcame a challenge. What did you learn about your potential through that experience?*
- *Write about someone you admire for their courage and potential. What qualities do they have that you can bring into your own life?*

2. Action Plan Pages

The "Action Plan" sections are essential to help readers turn their reflections into steps toward personal growth. Here's a template for the action pages:

Action Plan: Embracing Authenticity

- **What is one small way you can show up more authentically in your life this week?**
    - *Example*: Speak your truth in a conversation with a loved one.
    - **My Action**: _____
- **What fears are holding you back from expressing your true self?**
    - *Example*: Fear of rejection, fear of not being accepted.
    - **My Fears**: _____
- **How will you manage these fears and move forward anyway?**
    - *Example*: Take small steps, surround myself with supportive people.
    - **My Plan**: _____

Action Plan: Honouring My Self-Worth

- **What is one way you will practice self-compassion this week?**
    - *Example*: Speak kindly to myself in moments of doubt.
    - **My Action:** _____
- **How can you ensure your boundaries are respected moving forward?**
    - *Example*: Have a conversation with a friend about my limits.
    - **My Action:** _____
- **What can you do to remind yourself of your worth each day?**
    - *Example*: Read affirmations, journal about my strengths.
    - **My Action:** _____

Action Plan: Stepping Into Your Full Potential

- **What's one area of your life where you'd like to grow or take a risk?**
    - *Example*: I want to apply for that job I've been eyeing but feel unqualified for.
    - **My Area:** _____
- **What's one small step you can take this week to move toward that goal?**
    - *Example*: Update my resume, start gathering the necessary documents.
    - **My Step:** _____
- **Who can support you in reaching this goal?**
    - *Example*: A mentor, a friend, a support group.
    - **My Support:** _____

3. Affirmations

Affirmations can serve as a daily reminder of one's worth and potential. Here are a few, grouped by theme, for readers to write or say aloud daily:

Authenticity Affirmations

- "I am enough just as I am."
- "I trust myself to make decisions that align with my true self."
- "I embrace my uniqueness and celebrate my authenticity."
- "Every day, I become more comfortable in my own skin."

Self-Worth Affirmations

- "I am worthy of love, respect, and success."
- "I give myself permission to take up space and exist fully."
- "I am deserving of healthy relationships that honour my value."
- "My worth is not defined by the opinions or actions of others."

Potential Affirmations

- "I am capable of achieving my dreams and goals."
- "I trust in my ability to handle whatever comes my way."
- "My potential is limitless, and I am ready to step into it."
- "Each day is a new opportunity to grow and embrace my greatness."

4. Worksheets or Exercises

Incorporating these mini exercises into the workbook will help readers not only reflect but also engage physically with the content.

Vision Board Exercise

1. What do you want to manifest in your life in the next 6 months to a year?
2. Create a vision board or collage using magazines, online images, or drawings. Include images and words that represent your goals, dreams, and the future you desire.
3. List 3 actions you can take to bring this vision to life:
    -
        1. _____
    -
        2. _____
    -
        3. _____

Goal-Setting Worksheet

1. **What is your primary goal for the next month?**
   - *Example*: "I want to begin setting boundaries in my relationships."
   - **My Goal**: _____
2. **Break it down into actionable steps.**
   - *Step 1*: _____
   - *Step 2*: _____
   - *Step 3*: _____
3. **How will you track your progress?**
   - *Example*: "I will check in with myself every week to see how I'm honouring my boundaries."
   - **Tracking Method**: _____
4. **What's the biggest obstacle you anticipate in achieving this goal?**
   - **Obstacle**: _____
5. **How will you overcome that obstacle?**
   - **Solution**: _____

---

5. Inspirational Quotes

Here are a few motivational quotes that can be strategically placed throughout the workbook to keep your readers inspired:

- *"Your task is not to seek for love, but merely to seek and find all the barriers within yourself that you have built against it."* - Rumi
- *"You are the only person who can limit your greatness."* - Anonymous
- *"The journey of a thousand miles begins with one step."* - Lao Tzu
- *"Don't wait for the perfect moment, take the moment and make it perfect."* - Anonymous

6. Interactive Checkpoints

These checkpoints will help readers assess their emotional state and help them recalibrate if they're feeling stuck or overwhelmed. You can include these at key points in the workbook.

Checkpoint 1: Midway Reflection

- **How do you feel right now?**
  - *Example: Do you feel excited? Anxious? Empowered? Or maybe stuck? Write about your current emotional state.*
- **What is one thing you're struggling with, and how can you shift your mindset or perspective on it?**
- **What small victory have you experienced so far that deserves recognition?**

Checkpoint 2: Ready for Action

- **Are you ready to take the next step? If so, what is it?**
- **What is the biggest obstacle standing in your way right now?**
  - *Example: Fear, uncertainty, lack of resources... Write about how you can move past this.*

7. Accountability Partner or Group

Encouraging readers to share their journey can increase their sense of community and provide valuable support. A reminder for accountability could look something like this:

Accountability Partner Tips

- *Find someone you trust to share your progress with. This could be a friend, a coach, or even a member of an online support group. Tell them about your goals, struggles, and victories. Make sure they know how they can best support you in this process!*
- *Set up a weekly check-in where you share your action steps and hold each other accountable.*

Workbook Outline: "Embracing Your Authentic Self: A Journey to Self-Worth and Potential"

Introduction: Welcome to Your Transformation

- **Purpose of the Workbook:**
  A brief introduction to explain the journey the reader will take through this workbook. This section should include an invitation to take the time to reflect, engage with the exercises, and approach the process with an open heart and mind.

  Example: "This workbook is designed to guide you through a process of rediscovery and empowerment. It will help you tap into your authentic self, honour your worth, and unlock your full potential. Let's embark on this journey of transformation together."

Section 1: Embracing Authenticity

Objective: To help the reader connect with their true self and discover what it feels like to live authentically.

---

1. **Introduction to Authenticity**
   A few paragraphs defining what authenticity means and why it's crucial for personal growth and happiness.
2. **Journaling Prompts for Authenticity**
   - *What does being authentic mean to you? Describe a time when you felt completely yourself.*
   - *What are the areas in your life where you feel most inauthentic? Why do you think that is?*
3. **Action Plan: Embracing Authenticity**
   - **What is one small way you can show up more authentically this week?**
     - *My Action:* _____
   - **What fears hold you back from expressing your true self?**
     - *My Fears:* _____
   - **How will you manage these fears?**
     - *My Plan:* _____
4. **Affirmations for Authenticity**
   - "I trust myself to make decisions that align with my true self."
   - "I embrace my uniqueness and celebrate my authenticity."
5. **Exercise: Vision Board for Authenticity**
   - **What are your most important values?**
     - *My Values:* _____

- Create a visual representation of what living authentically looks like to you. Use images, words, or symbols that resonate with your truth.
    - *Attach your vision board or sketch it here:*

6. **Checkpoint**:
    - How do you feel about your authenticity right now?
        - *Check-in Emotion*: _____
        - *What is one way you can reinforce your authentic self today?*

Section 2: Honouring Your Self-Worth

Objective: To help readers explore their sense of self-worth, uncover limiting beliefs, and establish practices for valuing themselves.

---

1. **Introduction to Self-Worth**
   Discuss the importance of recognizing one's inherent value, separate from external validation or approval.
2. **Journaling Prompts for Self-Worth**
    - *Think about a time you accepted less than you deserved. How did that impact you?*

- o *What are three things that make you feel worthy of love and respect?*
3. **Action Plan: Honouring Your Self-Worth**
    - o **What is one way you will practice self-compassion this week?**
        - *My Action*: _____
    - o **How can you ensure your boundaries are respected moving forward?**
        - *My Action*: _____
    - o **What can you do to remind yourself of your worth every day?**
        - *My Action*: _____
4. **Affirmations for Self-Worth**
    - o "I am worthy of love, respect, and success."
    - o "I honour my boundaries and respect my needs."
    - o "My worth is inherent, and I don't need to prove it."
5. **Exercise: Self-Worth Challenge**
    - o For the next 7 days, commit to one action that reinforces your self-worth each day. This could be setting a boundary, speaking up for yourself, or practicing self-compassion.
    - o **Track your progress**:
        - Day 1: _____
        - Day 2: _____
        - Day 3: _____
        - *Continue for a week*

6. **Checkpoint**:
    - o How are you honouring your self-worth right now?

- *Check-in Emotion:* _____

- **What area of your life still needs work in terms of honouring your worth?**

Section 3: Unlocking Your Full Potential

Objective: To help the reader recognize their true potential and start taking action toward their biggest goals and dreams.

---

1. **Introduction to Potential**
   This section should motivate the reader to see that they are capable of achieving more than they often realize, and that their potential is limitless.
2. **Journaling Prompts for Potential**
   - *What is a dream or goal you've put off due to fear or doubt? What would it take for you to move toward it today?*
   - *When you look back on your life, what do you want to have achieved?*
3. **Action Plan: Stepping Into Your Potential**
   - **What's one area of your life where you want to take a risk?**
     - *My Goal:* _____
   - **What small steps can you take this week to move toward your goal?**
     - *My Action Steps:* _____
4. **Affirmations for Potential**
   - "I am capable of achieving all that I set my mind to."
   - "I trust my intuition to guide me to my highest potential."

- "My potential is limitless, and I am worthy of living the life I dream of."
5. **Exercise: Goal-Setting Worksheet**
    - **My primary goal for the next month is:**
      _____

    - **Break this goal down into actionable steps:**
      - Step 1: _____
      - Step 2: _____
      - Step 3: _____
6. **Checkpoint:**
    - **Are you ready to take action on your potential?**
      - *Check-in Emotion:*
        _____

      - **What's the biggest obstacle standing in your way?**
      - **How will you overcome that obstacle?**

Final Reflection: Your Journey Forward

- **Looking Back, Moving Forward**
  Encourage readers to reflect on how far they've come and how they can continue using the tools from the workbook in their everyday life.

  Prompt: "What's the biggest shift you've noticed in yourself since starting this workbook? How can you keep this momentum going in the weeks and months to come?"

- **Celebration:**
  Celebrate their journey, reminding them that transformation is a continuous process. Offer words of encouragement and remind them that they now have the tools to continue living

authentically, honouring their worth, and stepping into their potential.

Conclusion: Continuing the Journey

- **What's next for you?**
  Encourage readers to continue exploring and using the tools provided. Offer additional resources such as books, pod casts, or communities they can join to stay on track.

Additional Notes

- **Visuals:** You can also consider including some illustrations, icons, or simple design elements to break up the text and make the workbook more visually engaging.
- **Resources:** Add a section at the end for any additional resources, books, websites, or online communities that support the themes of authenticity, self-worth, and personal growth.

Phenomenal Women - "How I Lost Myself – And Found the Fire to Rise Again"

By Donn C. McCalla

Reflective Workbook: Embracing Your Journey of Transformation

This workbook is your space to integrate, reflect, and act. Use the prompts, affirmations, and exercises below to deepen your healing journey and reclaim your voice.

Journaling Prompts

Journaling Prompts
- What are the three biggest obstacles you've faced in standing in your truth?
- Reflect on a time when you were your most authentic self. How did that feel?
- Think about a moment when you put someone else's needs above your own. How did it impact you?

Daily Affirmations

Daily Affirmations

- ✧ I am worthy of love, respect, and peace.
- ✧ I trust myself and my inner wisdom.
- ✧ I honour my boundaries and protect my energy.
- ✧ My truth is valid, and I do not need permission to own it.
- ✧ I am not broken. I am rising.

Printed in Great Britain
by Amazon

5aecf708-f367-448b-a1fb-ef446c7b8ac0R01